Praying the Rosary

Praying the Rosary

NEW REFLECTIONS ON THE MYSTERIES

Gloria Hutchinson

ST.
ANTHONY
MESSENGER
PRESS

CINCINNATI, OHIO

Nihil Obstat: Rev. Thomas Richstatter, O.F.M.
          Rev. Robert J. Buschmiller

Imprimi Potest: Rev. John Bok, O.F.M.
           Provincial

Imprimatur: +James H. Garland, V.G.
           Archdiocese of Cincinnati
           August 9, 1991

The *nihil obstat* and *imprimatur* are a declaration that a book is considered to be free from doctrinal or moral error. It is not implied that those who have granted the *nihil obstat* and *imprimatur* agree with the contents, opinions or statements expressed.

Scripture citations are taken from *The New Jerusalem Bible,* published and copyright ©1985 by Darton, Longman and Todd Ltd. and Doubleday and Co. Inc., and are used by permission of the publishers. Passage from *Mary, Wellspring of Peace* by Joan Chittister, O.S.B., used by permission of Pax Christi U.S.A., 348 East Tenth Street, Erie, Penna. 16503. Passage from *How Relevant Is the Bible?* by John L. McKenzie, S.J., used by permission of the Thomas More Press. Passages from *Silence* by Shusako Endom, copyright ©1969 by Monumenta Nipponica, reprinted by permission of Taplinger Publishing Co. Inc. Passages from *New Seeds of Contemplation* by Thomas Merton, copyright ©1971 by the Abbey of Gethsemani, used by permission of the Merton Legacy Trust. Passages from *The Asian Journal of Thomas Merton,* copyright ©1968, 1970, 1973 by the Trustees of the Merton Legacy Trust, used by permission of the Merton Legacy Trust. The quotation from *In Praise of Krishna,* ©1967 by the Asia Society, is adapted with permission of the translators, Edward C. Dimock, Jr., and Denise Levertov.

Cover and book design by Julie Lonneman

ISBN 0-86716-143-4

Published by St. Anthony Messenger Press

Contents

Introduction

She's a mystery. I only think I know her. Accustomed to book learning, I keep sifting for additional clues. There's not much to go on. In the entire New Testament, Mary speaks only five times; throughout Matthew and Mark, she remains silent. John respectfully mentions her twice. Despite his eye for the discipleship of women, Luke loses sight of her after Jesus makes his adolescent stand in the Temple. Can we blame biblical scholar John L. McKenzie, S.J., for concluding in *Is the Bible Relevant?* that "the Mary of popular belief is a fictitious character"?

We mold our images of Mary from the clay of Scripture, tradition and experience. Sometimes we mix in too much of one ingredient or another. But as long as the Mary who emerges is "the first and the most perfect of Christ's disciples," as Pope Paul VI called her, we needn't worry about creating a total counterfeit. I try to stay close to the Mary who takes risks, bears rejection, confronts the unjust, identifies with the poor, heartens the sick and guides the doubtful.

There's no denying that I often lose sight of her. It's easy to fall back against the old stereotypes of Mary as passive, submissive, self-effacing—the woman most modern women are struggling not to be. When that happens, I have to remember not to blame Mary for the distortions that have hidden her reality in the past.

When I pick up the rosary, I have to overcome an initial aversion to repetition in prayer. A little sleight of hand helps. I roll the round wooden beads slowly between thumb and forefinger, enjoying the tactile connection. The surfaces of the beads seem to communicate tranquillity. Gradually, I untangle my thoughts and set out on the circular path.

Mentally walking or riding also helps. I'm going somewhere with Mary: down memory lane; south to Bethlehem or some other birthplace; north to Jerusalem or a less distant sacrificial altar. The Hail Marys are the steps I take—often moving my feet to keep the prayer in progress. Each mystery is a way station where, if the journey is going well, I pause to rest, recollect and redirect my intentions.

Hurry drains the color from my rosary. I might as well have driven down the Maine coast without noticing the passing seascape. Madeleine L'Engle describes how the native Hawaiians used to sit for long periods outside their temples before they entered to pray and after they had made their petitions. They were "breathing life" into their prayers.

This book is an attempt to breathe life into the rosary for readers who, like me, are doing their post-Vatican II best to see how this traditional devotion relates to their contemporary lives. Each mystery begins with a personal Reflection linked in some way to the Mary-Jesus events. Readers, who are the cocreators of this book, are encouraged to substitute or spin off reflections from their own lives that echo the human experience of "The Finding," for instance, or "The Arising."

The second section of each mystery is a Meditation based on Scripture, tradition and the author's interpretation of the event. Each is a story of what happened and/or what might have happened when Jesus agonized in the garden, for instance, or when Mary was crowned Queen of Heaven by her Son. Again, readers are invited to make what they will of the stories. For a story is shaped as much by the listener's experience as by the storyteller's art.

Following the meditation is a brief Response. Here readers must stop, slough off any remaining passivity, roll up their sleeves and do the work of making the rosary their own. Think. Remember. Connect. Pray. Act. Allow the rosary to pass not only through your fingers but into your body, into your being.

In these fifteen chapters, I have tried to breathe life into the rosary by taking time, making connections and wondering about Mary—always remembering that no disciple outranks her Teacher.

THE
JOYFUL
MYSTERIES

The Calling
◆ **ONE** ◆

REFLECTION The call came to me in my nineteenth summer. At first, I thought the Lord's signals had gotten crossed: I had already been accepted by a teaching order of Franciscan sisters when their librarian sent me a book called *A Right to be Merry*. Written by Sister Mary Francis, P.C.C., it described the daily life of the Poor Clare nuns of Our Lady of Guadalupe Monastery in Roswell, New Mexico.

As I read about the Clares' primitive rule and their strict observance of "holy poverty," I cringed in my chair and reached for another cup of coffee. "How can they stand it?" I wondered. "Getting up in the middle of the night to pray. Fasting. Keeping silent. Remaining walled off from the rest of the world. I'll bet some of them go stir-crazy. Unreal."

Oddly enough, I felt compelled to read the book a

second time. The austerities sounded a bit less daunting and the contemplative life no longer pure drudgery. By the third reading, I had burrowed deep enough to catch the scent of the Poor Clares' selfless spirituality and dedication to Christ.

That's when I recognized the call. Could anyone but the Spirit make almost total abnegation alluring? My relatives and friends tried to deter me. Some decided I had gone off the deep end and become "a religious freak." But I had heard the invitation ("Come apart with me" [see Mark 6:31]) and no rational argument could stop me from saying, "I'm on my way."

For me, the Poor Clares were the answer to a youthful dream of perfection this side of paradise. They would mother the seed of contemplation within me, guiding into the light that which had been hidden in darkness.

MEDITATION Mary must have been 14 or 15 when her calling came. As a devout Jew, she would have spent long hours praying and dreaming about the coming Messiah. Who is to say that she had not, in some moment of soaring inspiration, envisioned herself as the mother of the Holy One? Perhaps the persistent fire within her drew the Lord God like the incense at Yom Kippur.

On a morning green with promise, she is seated in the walled courtyard of her home in Nazareth. She breathes as lightly as a sleeping sparrow so that no sound intrudes on her awareness of Yahweh's presence. The perfect stillness of her mind is communicated by the immobility of her body: stillness, perfect stillness.

Gradually Mary becomes mindful of the presence of

another in the courtyard. She opens her eyes. There before her is a being not made of flesh but of light. She has never seen such commanding beauty before. Not even King David, whom she often envisions, could have looked like this. The figure bows slightly to her, saying, "Rejoice, you who enjoy God's favor!" (Luke 1:28b).

She catches her breath. Her eyes widen to take in the messenger's radiance. "The Lord is with you" (Luke 1:28c), he announces, as though he were paying his respects to a queen. The quiescent waters of Mary's contemplation are disturbed. She wonders, *What does this mean? Am I caught up in a vision? Enlighten me, Lord.*

Gabriel discerns her uncertainty and assures her. "Mary, do not be afraid. You have won God's favor. Look! You are to conceive in your womb and bear a son, and you must name him Jesus. He will be great and will be called Son of the Most High" (Luke 1:30-32a).

She wavers, confounded by his announcement. Is it possible? Has she been chosen for the highest honor any Israelite woman could desire? Her lips part but no sound emerges. Gabriel stands poised for her response. *Son of the Most High! Son of the Most High!* Mary cannot hear the words enough. They promise that the interminable waiting of her people will soon be over. The reign of justice is on the horizon.

"The Lord God will give him the throne of his ancestor David; he will rule over the House of Jacob forever and his reign will have no end" (Luke 1:32b-33), Gabriel promises.

The Messiah is coming! He is coming through me! But Mary's mind fastens on the reality of motherhood, and doubt drags her down the mountain. She and Joseph, her betrothed, have not given full expression to their love. How is a virgin to conceive?

"But how can this come about, since I have no knowledge of man?" (Luke 1:34b).

"The Holy Spirit will come upon you and the power of the Most High will cover you with its shadow. And so the child will be holy and will be called Son of God" (Luke 1:35).

Before Mary can speak her wonder, Gabriel offers her a sign authenticating his message. Her aged and barren cousin Elizabeth is now six months pregnant, "for nothing is impossible to God" (Luke 1:37). Elizabeth, who has been the object of other women's pity, will now be the envy of them all. Mary looks fearlessly into the angel's face and says, "You see before you the Lord's servant, let it happen to me as you have said" (Luke 1:38b).

Satisfied, Gabriel salutes her and disappears from her sight. When she emerges from awe, Mary revels in a joy of rare vintage. Later the questions will claim her (*How can I tell Joseph? Will he leave me? Will my parents believe me? What will the neighbors say? Might I be stoned as an adulteress?*). For now, she belongs to joy. Taking down her braid, she whirls around the courtyard, keeping time to the melody of a triumphant psalm.

RESPONSE The Annunciation reminds us of how unexpectedly and inexplicably God breaks into our lives, intervenes in our plans, upsets our applecarts. God may speak to us through a person, a book, a place, a dream—an angel, if we have eyes for one.

Reflect on a time of annunciation in your own life. Ask Mary to direct your thoughts about how faithful you have been to the message you received. Seek her help in becoming more receptive to God's intervention in your life.

The Sharing
◆ TWO ◆

REFLECTION Although my Poor Clare calling proved to be only for a time, the contemplative life has continued its claim on me in nonmonastic forms. Years later our diocesan newspaper sent me on a pilgrimage to Lourdes. At that point my devotion to Mary was as vigorous as a poinsettia that's been forgotten in the basement. But I hoped the pilgrimage might lead me to a more mature relationship with our Lady.

Many of my fellow pilgrims were severely disabled or terminally ill. Observing the transformation they went through during our eight days at the shrine opened my eyes to Mary as a source of consolation and healing. I saw how her maternal influence motivated people with disabilities to compassion for each other, inspired gratitude and service in the healthy and planted hope in hearts that had been dried up by misery.

After the pilgrimage, I wanted to witness to Mary's intercessory power. For years I had been a secular journalist and had shied away from any written expression of my faith. But now Mary kept nudging me on until I had completed a book of meditations on her healing influence.

When the first slender copy of that literary child arrived, I was delighted and uncertain. With whom could I share it before it was revealed to the public? Who would reassure me that my offspring was a gift from the Lord? Who better than my close friend Barbara, a beginning poet and an inquirer into relationship with Mary herself!

The 10-mile trip to her house seemed endless that day. Her joy at seeing my first book, however, somehow made the accomplishment seem more real, more meaningful, like a secret that is without value until it is shared with someone.

MEDITATION As the embryonic Son begins to take form in her womb, Mary has to tell someone, has to share her joy and her fear of discovery. She cannot bring herself to tell Joseph just yet. And the truth might prove too great a burden for her parents. There is only one person she can tell, one who can understand God's mysterious way of working within her. She will make the journey to Ain Farah, saying only that she wants to visit her cousin Elizabeth, whom she has not seen in a long time.

During the long trek into the hill country of Judah with a party of distant relatives, she is often tempted to tell her good news. But discretion advises silence. These friendly kinsmen might promptly turn against her for impugning the family's honor.

When Mary arrives at the home of Zechariah and Elizabeth, anticipation wipes out the fatigue of her journey. Now her woman's heart can unburden itself without fear of rejection or ridicule. She brushes the dust from her tunic and looks up to see Elizabeth walking slowly toward her, moving with a liturgical solemnity as though she were a high priest bearing the Ark of the Covenant.

"Elizabeth! My dear Elizabeth!" Mary says, quickening her pace. At the sound of Mary's voice, Elizabeth gasps with pain and pleasure. Instinctively she pats her stomach as though to calm the wild prophet-child gamboling within. Then, invaded by the Spirit-wind, she cries out in confidence, "Of all women you are the most blessed, and blessed is the fruit of your womb. Why should I be honored with a visit from the mother of my Lord?" (Luke 1:42).

Tears of relief wash over Mary's face as she embraces her friend. "How did you know?" she whispers, resting her cheek on Elizabeth's shoulder. "Look, the moment your greeting reached my ears, the child in my womb leaped for joy. Yes, blessed is she who believed that the promise made her by the Lord would be fulfilled" (Luke 1:44-45), Elizabeth answers.

Then the tears of both women mingle in a stream of gladness. They cling to each other for long moments while their unborn sons press against each other like lion cubs nestling.

Later, while the cousins recline at the table, Mary narrates the story of her encounter with the angel. She leisurely embroiders in the multihued details, enjoying the luxury of Elizabeth's attention. In the telling, she feels herself gathering strength and courage. Frequently, she reaches across the table to clasp Elizabeth's hands. "Oh my friend, my sister, how good it is for us to be pregnant together! The Almighty has blessed us beyond all women. Can you believe that the Messiah is here with us at this moment? Can you believe it, dear sister?"

"Nothing is impossible with God, Mary. Look at us. We

are living proof of God's power!"

As one, they break into laughter that echoes in the ears of the coming Messiah and his impatient herald. Rejoicing rumbles through the house and rises to the heavens. Captivated by the music of feminine elation, Yahweh smiles on his faithful daughters.

RESPONSE Search your memory for a time when you were bursting to tell some secret good news, intuition or discovery. Who was your Elizabeth and why? How did this visitation affect you? Did it, in any way, affirm your identity?

Call on Mary to deepen any soul-friendships you now have, or to guide you into a new relationship of spiritual sharing.

The Bringing Forth
◆ THREE ◆

REFLECTION I've always marveled at those women who say, "The moment I saw my baby's face, I forgot about all the pain I'd been through." For me, labor was not a forgettable experience. It remains as fresh in my memory as the farewell scene ("Frankly, my dear, I don't give a damn") from *Gone With the Wind*.

It was Christmas night and the obstetrician on duty in

the Air Force hospital was a Jewish doctor I'd never seen before. My own physician, a Christian, was at home with his family. I was confined among strangers whose uninhibited screams warned me I had something to dread. The nurse's crisp little comments about "not getting all tensed up" irked me. I wanted to crack some wry joke in response. But a spasm caught me and I cried out instead.

Never before had I so completely understood the helplessness of the human condition. For six hours I was at the mercy of an interior tide that swept me along like defenseless flotsam. Whenever I was rational enough to put two or three words together, I would pray "Lord, help me" or "Let my baby be born soon."

When our son finally came wailing and kicking into this world, I did not forget the pain of his coming. But I counted it a small price to pay for the life I now held gently, gently in my hands. His face, miraculously tiny and creased like old leather, was a thing of beauty to be marveled at and cried over. We named him David because he was "beloved."

MEDITATION "So Joseph set out from the town of Nazareth in Galilee for Judea, to the town of David called Bethlehem, since he was of David's house and line, in order to be registered with Mary, his betrothed, who was with child" (Luke 2:4-5).

Joseph does his best to make her comfortable on a bed of straw. She has endured the jolting ride from Nazareth and the rude shock of "no room" without complaint. He wishes her mother could have come with them to attend her. "Miryam, my Miryam," he says. "Forgive me for not

providing a more fitting place for you. You have been so
brave and I have given you so little in return. Why couldn't
the census have come at a better time?"

"Shush, my darling Joseph. It is God's will that we
should be together in this place. I could not ask for a softer
bed or a more loving companion," Mary responds.

Joseph tucks the woolen blanket around her. He strokes
her hair and hums her favorite melodies for distraction.
When her labor begins, Mary grasps his calloused hands
and tries to smile his worries away. "All will be well,
Joseph," she assures him. "Pray with me now, for this
precious child is preparing to emerge." Together husband
and wife pray heart-known verses from Isaiah depicting the
Messiah who is to come. Whenever Mary's voice falters or
she gives way to groaning, Joseph redoubles his devotion.

"...[W]hile they were there, the time came for her to
have her child, and she gave birth to a son, her
firstborn"(Luke 1:7b). Mary labors in sweat and agony
until the child emerges into Joseph's trembling hands. With
a cry, the infant announces his presence; his clenched fists
part the air as though clearing a way through the crowd for
a mighty king. As one, Mary and Joseph laugh in
admiration.

Whatever the cost of bringing him forth, Mary knows,
with one look at his redly-wrinkled infant-Savior face, that
she will never again experience the pure joy of their first
few hours together—hours when Emmanuel belongs not to
the world but to his mother.

The Messiah is flesh of her flesh. His curly black hair,
still damp from her womb, is her hair. His black eyes,
squinting up at her, are dark mirrors of her own. His
irresistible baby smell fills her senses and surpasses the

finest frankincense. She cuddles him to her breast and knows that she is more exalted than the Herods or the high priests.

"She wrapped him in swaddling clothes and laid him in a manger..." (Luke 1:6-7a). Then Mary and Joseph kneel beside the golden child who is the world's peace. Laughingly, they take turns kissing his rosy soft head and embracing one another.

RESPONSE Call to mind a nativity experience in which you brought forth a new life that gave you joy: a child, a work of art or craft, a friendship, a special liturgy, a healing or reconciliation, some sign of God's creative power working through you. Ask Mary to increase your appreciation of the creative act, which often requires a dying to ourselves, a painful laboring, a long preparation. Seek her intercession in recognizing what new life you are now called to bring forth.

The Giving
♦ FOUR ♦

REFLECTION One home liturgy I'll never forget was celebrated by a group of Maine artisans who call themselves "Body Works" because they believe that their works build up the Body of Christ. At the presentation of the gifts, to the simple melody "Of My Hands," the artisans offered their creations to the Lord. Two weavers presented a lovely blue *talith* or prayer shawl with white tassels, a shawl symbolizing the common bond of scriptural prayer between Christians and Jews. A potter offered an earthenware chalice which had so pleased her that she vowed never again to make anything but liturgical vessels. A carpenter placed before the altar-table a smoothly-crafted set of paddles for canoeing, which he experienced as a contemplative act. Inscribed silver crosses, religious books and scriptural illustrations were lovingly placed at the Lord's feet.

Each work represented weeks or months of labor, frustration and striving for perfection. Each was a visible prayer from the hearts and hands of its maker. "What you have given us, Spirit-Lord, we give back to you with grateful hearts. May our gifts grow and prosper for your glory," the artisans prayed.

MEDITATION When Mary and Joseph go up to the Temple with the infant Jesus in their arms, they are prepared to return to God the greatest gift given them. As faithful Jews, they consecrate to Yahweh their firstborn son in gratitude for deliverance from Egypt. "All human firstborn, however, those of your own race, you will redeem. And when your son asks you in days to come, 'What does this mean?' you will tell him, 'By the strength of his hand Yahweh brought us out of Egypt, out of the place of slave-labor. When Pharaoh stubbornly refused to let us go, Yahweh killed all the firstborn in Egypt, of man and of beast alike" (Exodus 13:14-15).

The presentation of Jesus arouses Mary's pride and joy in the son, who becomes more beautiful to her with every passing day. While the priest conducts the hallowed ritual of consecration, Mary prays, "Adonai, here is your Son whom you entrusted to me. Gladly I give him back to you, recognizing your prior and eternal claim on him. Help me to care for and guide him. Remind me not to possess or constrain. Let it be done to us as you will."

Is this "let it be done" more costly than the first? Now that she has held him, nursed him, rocked him, consoled him, can she really let go and say, "He's yours, not mine"? As she struggles with detachment, Mary encounters the venerable Simeon, who lifts Jesus on high like a sacrificial offering.

Mary stands, open-mouthed, wondering at Simeon's wisdom. His raven eyes fasten on her and she is held captive in his talons. "You see this child," he says, croaking with intensity. "Look, he is destined for the fall and for the rising of many in Israel, destined to be a sign that is opposed..." (Luke 2:34b). Simeon pauses. A shudder passes through Mary as she steps back to avoid the blow.

"And a sword will pierce your own soul too—so that the secret thoughts of many may be laid bare" (Luke 2:35). Joseph draws Mary to himself as though to shield her from the prophecy's fulfillment. She says nothing but mutely holds out her arms to receive her son. "Oh, my little son, my beloved! I will protect you. You are the joy of my life."

RESPONSE Recall an experience of presentation in your own life. As a parent, you may have offered your daughter or son to the Lord. You may have offered a ministry, a work of love, a virtue or a vow. Invite Mary into your reflection on how faithful you have been in preserving or renewing your offering. Ask her to teach you how to love without possessing, to guide without controlling. Lift up in the temple of your heart the one person for whom you most seek God's blessing.

The Finding
◆ FIVE ◆

REFLECTION I'll never forget that day on the beach. I looked up from the magazine I'd been reading, expecting to see my six-year-old son playing in the water where he had been for the past ten minutes or so. But David was nowhere in sight. A shot of adrenaline jolted me into action. I rushed into the water, turning in every direction to see if he had just wandered off a bit. I called his name loudly and asked everyone in the vicinity if they had seen him.

Suddenly, unbidden, the image of him drowning with no one to rescue him burst into my consciousness. I ran down the beach searching for the lifeguard. Bathers eyed me curiously as I bumped into them or ran over them. Panic made my heart pound and stole my breath. When I finally found the guard, I literally grabbed him and began dragging him down the beach. "Ma'am, try to calm down. We've never lost a child on this beach, believe me," he kept saying.

By the time we reached my blanket, I was beside myself with anxiety and exhaustion. Then I saw David, sitting quietly, building a sand castle as though nothing had happened. Laughing, the lifeguard patted my arm and said, "You see? I told you he had just wandered off."

I was speechless. Should I run up and hug my son, saying, "Thank God, you're all right"? Or should I shake the dickens out of him and say, "How could you do that to me? I was worried to death!" In a split second, I decided on the former. But I never got over the fear of losing my son.

M E D I T A T I O N Mary is distraught when she discovers that her son is not with the large party of neighbors and relatives journeying home from Jerusalem. She alternately blames herself for granting him too much independence and her extended family for being lax in looking after him. She rushes from one to another, interrogating with increasing anxiety: "When did you see him last? Who was he with? Didn't you notice his absence?"

Allowing themselves only a few hours' rest each night, Mary and Joseph hurry back toward the Holy City, filled with unnerving speculations about what might have happened to Jesus if he had fallen in with unsavory pilgrims or thieves. "We will go straight to the Temple, Joseph," Mary says. "Remember how he loves to sit and listen to the priests and scribes whenever we come here? Ever since he was a small boy, he has always spoken of the Temple with shining eyes and eager questions."

And when they found him, addressing the elders in the courtyard, discoursing with the air of a young rabbi, Mary and Joseph are overcome with relief and joy. They stand for a few moments, silently watching him, assuring themselves that it is indeed their Jesus, their beloved son.

Mary is torn between the desire to embrace and the need to recriminate. She feels that it is her parental right and duty to question him: "My child, why have you done this to us? See how worried your father and I have been, looking for you" (Luke 2:48b).

His cool detachment takes her by surprise, causing sudden tears. "Why were you looking for me? Did you not know that I must be in my Father's house?" (Luke 2:49a) he asks. She does not understand and is too tired to cope with perplexity. He smiles to reassure her and says to the elders, "I must go now. My parents have come for me."

All the way home Mary ponders his words and their implications. She restrains the desire to hang onto him, fold him under her wing. But she never for a moment lets him out of her sight.

RESPONSE Recall an important experience of loss (by death or disappearance, a broken relationship, a misguided choice) and consider how it has changed you. Have you ever "lost Jesus" and found him again by selfless searching?

Call on Mary to help you integrate these experiences into your faith life so they may nurture growth and wisdom.

THE
SORROWFUL MYSTERIES

Accepting the Cup
◆ ONE ◆

REFLECTION The night we saw *Romero* the theater was nearly empty. We huddled in our winter jackets, shuffling our feet like soft-shoe vaudevillians. We should have complained to the management. But to mention a small discomfort while observing so terrible a trial by fire would have shamed us. In the presence of El Salvador's suffering, hardly magnified on the vast curve of screen, we knew our own inadequacy as First World Christians.

Afterwards what haunted me was not the murder-at-the-altar scene. There the mingling of the Blood of the Lamb and the blood of the celebrant was too symbolically perfect; I felt the beauty of it more than Romero's pain. What I remembered was the man's excruciating agony of conscience, long, drawn out, fought against and finally obeyed. Like many of us, Oscar Romero had much to lose.

He had enjoyed the reputation of a good priest, a spiritual scholar, an urbane dinner guest cultivated by the wealthy conservatives who ruled El Salvador. He burrowed in the den of political and ecclesiastical approval.

But the brutal murder of Father Rutilio Grande and other young priests who had taken as their own the cause of the poor ousted the Archbishop from his complacency. He could not remain "a frightened mouse of a man" and face himself in the mirror or face his God in the Eucharist. Reluctantly he began to ask questions, to make complaints, to issue warnings. Sometimes his voice trembled when he confronted the powerful who had been his patrons; at times he retreated before the soldiers and their machine guns.

As the atrocities against his priests and his people multiplied, Romero wept with anguish at his impotence. Nightmares pummeled him. He dreaded the direction in which God was undeniably leading him. Death threats were murmured. Yet the Archbishop did not refuse the cup that was offered. "I would be lying if I said I don't have an instinct for my own preservation," he said, "but persecution is a sign that we are on the right road."

For Oscar Romero, the right road would lead to Calvary. But what made his extraordinary martyrdom possible was the three years he spent in Gethsemane wrestling with the Angel of Death.

MEDITATION The Son of Mary enters the Garden, accompanied by his most reliable companions. His pulse has slowed considerably since the last cup of wine was shared. Having experienced communion with his friends so intensely, he is invulnerable. What real harm can come to

him? The disciples are his rampart; their rough bodies lean
against him, hover over him, jostle against him. He knows
that, wherever he is, his mother holds him securely in
memory and prayer. Most importantly, the Father is there,
inside heart and skull. Jesus is not alone.

Recalling how much they have been through, he advises
all but Peter, James and John to get some rest. Then he
withdraws farther into the shadows to pray. The night
silence flows through his skin, floods his brain. His
comforting thoughts have gone to sea. Cold vapors of fear
and distress prowl within. Shocked at how easily his
defenses have been penetrated, Jesus confides in the three:
"My heart is sorrowful to the point of death. Wait here, and
stay awake with me" (Matthew 26:38b).

He can still count on these three dearest ones. They will
not allow him to be swept away. Determined that all will be
well, he throws himself on the ground, prostrate in his
sonship, appealing to the Father. "Abba, Father!...For you
everything is possible" (Mark 14:36a). Cannot salvation be
accomplished in some other way? Must saving always be
linked with losing? Who knows what three more years of
persuasion might yield?

"Take this cup away from me" (Mark 14:36b), he prays.
Never before has his voice betrayed that subtly powerful
blend of pleading and commanding in prayer. Recognizing
the need for self-preservation, Jesus presses his face to the
earth in submission. "But let it be as you, not I, would have
it" (Matthew 26:39b).

Now he needs his companions more than ever.
Especially Peter, the broad-shouldered parental one. Peter
will embrace him and swear to stand by him come what
may. But the three are sleeping, sprawled on the ground

like children after a long day of roughhousing. He shakes
Peter to attention. "So you had not the strength to stay
awake with me for one hour? Stay awake and pray not to be
put to the test" (Matthew 26:40b-41a), Jesus warns. It pains
him to see that vulnerable look on the disciple's face. Is this
the rampart he relies on? Pity for those who have loved him
at the cost of jeopardizing their own lives then moves him
to add, "The spirit is willing enough, but human nature is
weak" (Matthew 26:41b).

And nature has its share in the Son of Mary. His roots
are tangled deep in the lives of Galilean fishermen,
Palestinian zealots, Judean farmers, women of Nazareth
and Bethany and Jerusalem. Memories of laughing children
who have crawled on his lap and lisped in his ear bind him
to the life of the beloved rabbi. Again, he withdraws and
prays: "My Father,...if this cup cannot pass by, but I must
drink it, your will be done!" (Matthew 26:42b).

He is already paying in blood for that excruciating
prayer. The sight of it pooling on his skin, then slowly
spilling onto the ground horrifies him. For an instant, he is
a child longing for his mother's voice, her ministering
touch. Then his will to obey returns, stronger and more
certain. When he finds his trusted friends asleep, this time
he simply says, "It will have to do." Jesus knows the
faltering of good intentions; he accepts the measured pace
of his friends' conversion.

At the fearful sound of an approaching crowd, he rouses
the disciples. The hour has come and they must stand with
him. Already his body is inwardly rebelling against the
poisonous taste of betrayal. His hands impulsively reach
for Peter and John. "Look, the hour has come when the Son
of Man is to be betrayed into the hands of sinners"

(Matthew 26:45b). His voice trembles as he steps forward to confront the powerful.

RESPONSE Reflect on a time of agony or intense anxiety in your life. How were you able to pass through your dread or fear? Consider how focusing on Jesus in Gethsemane might help you to accept the cup of suffering whenever life seems totally beyond your control. Call on Mary to "stay awake" with you in times of testing. Ask her to keep before your eyes the witness of Oscar Romero who prayed the rosary nightly and lived Mary's prayer: "Let it be...."

Enduring the Lash
◆ TWO ◆

REFLECTION When I first read about Dr. Sheila Cassidy, I was envious. She had done it all. As a mission doctor in Chile, she was tortured and imprisoned for treating a wounded revolutionary. After her release, she entered a Benedictine monastery and lived as a contemplative nun for eighteen months. She then embraced poverty in a simple life-style that ruled out such luxuries as washers, dryers and TVs. Finally, she returned to the practice of medicine as director of a small hospice where she ministers to the dying.

It took me awhile to realize that each path of discipleship had caused Sheila Cassidy great suffering, both in the fulfilling and in the moving on. Her zeal and desire to be "a fitting sacrifice" denied her the contentment of knowing that she was in the right place. Not until middle age was she able to see clearly that medicine was her authentic vocation, and that she did not have to return to the perils of South America for that vocation to be worthy in God's eyes.

It was her eight weeks' imprisonment in 1975, however, that confirmed Cassidy in her dedication to God's will. Although the secret police in Santiago would have released her had she divulged the names of priests and nuns who had helped the revolutionaries, she would not do so. Instead she deliberately misled the police in order to protect their prey. In doing so, she made herself a candidate for redoubled torture.

Gagged, bound, stripped and beaten, Sheila Cassidy knew the helplessness of Christ in the hands of his persecutors. She was a participant in Christ's Passion. She knew God had not abandoned her, yet that knowledge did not spare her from any of the horror or humiliation of her captivity. It did not protect her from depression in solitary confinement or banish the fear that made coherent prayer impossible.

Although she had reasons to despise those who made her an innocent victim, Cassidy was relieved to discover that she did not hate them. She saw them as God saw them: prisoners of darkness who were shackled by evil. With sincerity, she was able to pray, "Father, forgive them, for they know not what they do" (see Luke 23:34). Christ's prayer of compassion liberated Sheila Cassidy from bitterness and despair. It united her with the scourged Prisoner in a bond that still prevails.

MEDITATION He cannot believe they have deserted him. To alleviate the pain, Jesus convinces himself that they will soon return with his mother, Magdalene, Mary and Martha. There is little they can do now that he is imprisoned in the praetorium. But surely his friends will be just outside Pilate's residence. Theirs will be the first faces he sees when he emerges, and he will drink deeply from the solace they offer.

Gazing directly at Pilate, the prisoner finds cause for hope. The procurator is uneasy; he knows the high priests have concocted the charges of blasphemy and subversion. "Are you the king of the Jews?" (John 18:33b). Pilate inquires. Jesus gives him an opening. "Do you ask this of your own accord, or have others said it to you about me?" (John 18:34b), he asks politely. But Pilate, stung by the prisoner's tone and commanding presence, retorts, "Am I a Jew?" (John 18:35b).

Understanding Pilate's fears, the prisoner explains that his kingdom "is not a kingdom of this world" (John 18:36b). If that were the case, his disciples would have put up a fight in Gethsemane. Pilate remains in his self-constructed fortress. "So, then, you are a king?" (John 18:37a), he persists. Jesus, knowing that the procurator has chosen captivity, complies. "It is you who say that I am a king. I was born for this, I came into the world for this, to bear witness to the truth..." (John 18:37b), he says. If Pilate had only committed himself to the truth, he would have heard Jesus' voice. But he has chosen darkness; truth has no meaning for him.

The procurator leads his prisoner out into the morning sun. A large crowd has gathered. Jesus tilts his head, trying to keep the sweat out of his eyes as he scans for familiar faces. Pilate makes one last attempt to free him by offering the crowd a choice between Jesus and Barabbas. "[W]ould you like me, then, to release for you the king of the Jews?" (John 18:39b), he shouts, recoiling in contempt at their mindless roar: "Not this man....but Barabbas" (John 18:40a).

Without ever finding his mother's stricken face among those who wept at the mob's verdict, Jesus is roughly taken away by the guards to an inner court. There, bound and stripped, he is whipped before and behind with the *flagellum*. As each lash finds its mark, the bone at the tip gouges the prisoner's flesh. At first he bears this slave's punishment in silence.

He remembers ruefully his proclamation in the synagogue when he yearned for the affirmation of his own townspeople. They had turned on him for claiming Isaiah's prophecy described his saving mission. Why was it he said he had come? "[T]o proclaim liberty to captives, release to those in prison" (Isaiah 61:2), he now repeats between lashes. Unable to help himself, Jesus cries out like one entrapped by mauling lions.

He tries to focus on his torturers. Does bestiality mask a fear of weakness, of impugned manhood, of failing in Roman invincibility? Is self-hatred projected onto the victim who can, without qualms, be brutalized? Like Pilate, the soldiers prefer death to the risks of becoming fully human.

Jesus pities them even as he shrinks from them. Soon

unconsciousness carries him beyond their grasp and he senses a comforting presence. A refrain from his childhood solaces him. "As a mother comforts her child...comforts her child...her child" (see Isaiah 66:13).

R E S P O N S E Call to mind manifestations of evil in the world today against which you feel helpless. It might be the scourge of child abuse and abortion, of starvation used as a political weapon, of medical aid denied to the dying, of apartheid abroad and racial hatred at home, of massive arms budgets and outbursts of war. Invoke Mary, prophetess of the Magnificat, mother of a political prisoner, to guide you in deciding how to act effectively against the evil you have identified.

Wearing the Crown
◆ THREE ◆

R E F L E C T I O N I count among my spiritual friends a certain Father Rodrigues. He, unfortunately, does not exist in person; he lives between the covers of Shusako Endo's novel *Silence*. That circumstance does not make him any less influential a companion on the way. No doubt there have been many like him since Christ commanded, "Go out to the whole world; proclaim the gospel to all creation" (Mark 16:15b). But Rodrigues is the one I know best, the one I turn to when conscience dictates a choice between worship and service to another.

Rodrigues is sent to Japan as a Jesuit missionary in the seventeenth century, a time of persecution when Christians were daily martyred. His mission is to serve the faithful in their underground communities and to find out whether a Jesuit provincial has apostasized. Rodrigues is a good priest who dreads the possibility that one day he might betray his Lord. He yearns to see the face of Christ, a face about which the Bible remains silent. "I am always fascinated by the face of Christ," he admits, "just like a man fascinated by the face of his beloved."

As the novel progresses, Rodrigues learns that he must entrust his life to others in order to survive—to others who may prove traitorous. He comes to realize that he must be as willing to die for the unworthy in his flock as he is for the true believers.

Rodrigues's ministry among the persecuted Japanese leads him to a new understanding of sin. It was not, he thinks, a simple matter of stealing or lying. "Sin is for one man to walk brutally over the life of another and to be quite oblivious of the wounds he has left behind."

After he has been imprisoned for practicing an outlawed religion, the priest is urged to apostasize by trampling on the *fumie* (a copper medallion of Christ's face attached to a plank). If he does not, several poor peasants will be tortured and left to die in a slow agony. Out of love for Christ and loyalty to the Church, Rodrigues at first refuses. But Ferreira (the former provincial) convinces him that Jesus himself would apostasize in order to save the condemned ones.

Heartbroken and filled with self-loathing for what he is

about to do, Rodrigues looks down at the fumie. "Before him is the ugly face of Christ, crowned with thorns and the thin, outstretched arms." In an act of love that costs him everything, the priest tramples on the face of his Beloved.

Whenever I reread these key scenes in *Silence*, I marvel at the depth and the consequences of Rodrigues's compassion. I remember singing during so many Holy Weeks, "O Sacred Head, surrounded/By crown of piercing thorn!" And I try to imagine what it would be like to join those who "revile and put to scorn" the thorn-crowned Christ.

Would I ever forgive myself? Would he ever forgive me—if I did not trample in order to save those others?

M E D I T A T I O N Someone is slapping his face to revive him. He quickly awakens to the diffuse pain of the scourging. Closing his eyes, he inwardly groans, "My Father, if it is possible..." (Matthew 26:42b).

A peremptory command severs his prayer. "On your feet, Nazarene! We aren't finished with you yet."

The procurator's soldiers yank him into a standing position, propping him against a courtyard wall while the entire cohort converges like a pack of wolves anticipating a kill. The prisoner knows he will not survive the lash a second time. He smiles wanly at the prospect of leaving the executioners empty-handed. Isaiah whispers to him, and Jesus repeats:

> Lord Yahweh comes to my help,
> this is why insult has not touched me,
> this is why I have set my face like flint

31

and know that I shall not be put to shame.
(Isaiah 50:7)

His customary self-possession is regained. He confronts the soldiers with a look that knows nothing of fear or supplication. Two of them strip off his clothing, mouthing insults about the pitiable state of Jewish royalty. A third soldier flourishes a scarlet military cloak, letting it fall dramatically over the prisoner's shoulders.

"Aha! Now you are beginning to look like a king. You lack only a crown to complete your attire."

Bitter laughter erupts from the cohort as a pair of soldiers step forward bearing a crown they have woven from thorn boughs. Thrusting it down rudely so that the cap of thorns penetrates Jesus' scalp and forehead, they then stick a scepter of reed in his right hand. Bowing and scraping, they begin to outdo one another in derision.

"Your majesty! How can we serve you?"

"We salute the king of the Jews!"

"We tremble at your feet, O mighty one!"

"Shall I readjust your crown, majesty?"

They fall on their knees before him, dishonoring him with malicious contempt. They spit at him and strike him about the head. One blackens his eyes while another tugs sharply at his beard. Wresting the reed from his hand, they repeatedly smite him on the head with it.

Jesus bears their hatred without retort. The weight of his head, punctured by scores of wounds, is almost insupportable. Blood has pooled and dries in the creases of his neck and shoulders. He is so disfigured he hardly looks human; he appears to be one whose wickedness is so great that no ordinary punishment can suffice as requital.

Making a supreme effort to remain clear-minded, the

prisoner breathes a prayer of gratitude that neither his mother nor his friends has witnessed this mock veneration. She, more than the others, would have been startled by the disfigurement of his face, a face she held to be the most radiant and valiant and beautiful of any woman's son. She could not have imagined the vituperation that had been heaped upon him. And she could not have forgiven it easily.

The travesty has played itself out. Few of the soldiers have the stomach to go on. Someone pulls the blood-soaked cloak from Jesus' shoulders, while another returns the prisoner's tunic. He is led outside in a procession that parodies his triumphant arrival in Jerusalem before the Passover.

Realizing that his loved ones may be among the pilgrims and rabble-rousers waiting outside the praetorium, Jesus lifts his thorn-crowned head and straightens his shoulders as much as he is able.

R E S P O N S E Call to mind some of the ways in which you have observed or experienced the mocking of another's human dignity: a child is ridiculed as "stupid" or "clumsy"; a woman derided as "fat and ugly" or "a whore"; blacks or Hispanics beaten because others don't like the color of their faces. Seek Mary's help in becoming more sensitive to any attitudes or habits you may have that "crown" others with expressions of disrespect or scorn. Resolve not to trample on the Christ in others.

Bearing the Cross
◆ FOUR ◆

REFLECTION The two of them appeared on a TV talk show. Geraldo plied them with questions in an attempt to arouse audience empathy with their plight. The young man was about 20, handsome, athletic and apparently healthy. Seated beside him was his mother, a well-groomed woman with more worry lines than her age required. The bond between them was visible in the slight tilt of her head in his direction, in his unobtrusive way of occasionally covering her hand with his.

As the result of an auto accident caused by a drunken driver two years earlier, Gil (not his real name) had awakened in the hospital, a stranger to himself. He stared at the two anxious faces hovering over him and had no idea that they belonged to his parents. The woman wept when it became clear that her only son was a victim of amnesia.

At first the doctors thought Gil's affliction might be temporary. His mother patiently tried to stock his brain with memories of childhood. But even the most appealing and significant anecdotes prompted no response. Each morning Gil had to pick up the burden of alienation. Each morning it broke his mother's heart.

His friends soon depleted their willingness to wait for a breakthrough. His teammates couldn't believe that he no longer knew how to pass a football. His girlfriend soon tired of dating someone who had misplaced every memory of what they had meant to each other.

Because Gil had to begin learning everything from how to tie his sneakers to how to do simple addition over again, kids at school ridiculed his stupidity. They could no longer connect with him. Some were certain that he could remember if he tried hard enough. Gradually, they gave up on Gil.

"His friends all abandoned him. They just turned away," his mother told the TV audience. She alone had stood by her son for the two years since his accident, helping him to carry the burden of his alien self. They had been through a series of doctors, tests, treatments, depressions, failed hopes.

"She wound up in a psychiatric hospital," Gil said, nodding at his mother. The woman beside him was silent. She had not come to harvest pity for herself. Her one care was that others should understand the injustice and terrible loneliness her son was suffering. "I beg you," she pleaded, "give him a chance."

M E D I T A T I O N The condemned man stumbles as the rough beam is thrust across his shoulders. Since his childhood, apprenticed at his father's side, he has been intimately acquainted with the heft and character of wood. He has lugged ceiling beams, hoisted fresh-hewn doors into place and delivered yokes to Galilean farmers. But the beam he carries now will not be used to build or plant; it has been chosen as the instrument of his death.

When he falls the first time, the wood lurches forward, scraping the skin from his shoulders and holding him down like a merciless opponent.

"Get up, scoundrel. This is no time to rest."

The guards haul him to his feet and readjust the beam, prodding him onward like a pack animal. Jesus hears the abusive voices of the bystanders, hungry for another's humiliation to alleviate their own treatment by Rome. The prisoner assures himself that among them a few must be silently praying for him. But their muteness intensifies his isolation.

With eyes closed against the crowd and blood trickling from his forehead, the condemned man suddenly stops. He is a fisherman who, battered and tossed by an angry sea, unexpectedly comes upon a sheltering cove. Someone is standing before him, parting the sea so that he may enter the cove.

Jesus leans forward. A cool hand touches his bruised face. Like fragrant ointment, the hand heals a bruised spirit. It is the balm Jeremiah sought in Gilead.

The soldier, struck by the force of the woman's grief, immediately steps back. Mother and Son behold one another. A lifetime of maternal devotion is communicated in the bend of her head. Her fierce desire to protect him is held in only by her conviction that he, as always, is in Yahweh's hands. The eagle, caught in the fowler's snare, may yet be released by One mightier than Caiaphas or Caesar.

Abandoned by his disciples, Jesus has not been deserted by this one who gave him life and in return received it, this one who was his follower even before she fully realized what discipleship would require of her, this one who now understands what she must do for him.

As her hand is balm for his wounds, so her voice is a recompense for the crowd's mockery: "Yeshua!"

Each knows the other's heart, bears the other's pain, intuits the indestructible seed of joy that is about to be sown.

The captain of the guards steps in, moving the woman out of the prisoner's path. Jesus straightens up and attempts to walk on. Renewed in spirit, he still cannot command his enervated body. A farmer, heading home from the fields, is pressed into service. Simon the Cyrenean, inwardly cursing his destiny, stares at the prisoner with contempt as the crossbeam is transferred. Jesus lifts his head in gratitude and Simon is converted by a dislocated smile.

Mary is rent by the sword of knowing that a stranger had to be forced to come to her Son's aid. But her eyes bless the Cyrenean for being there as the two captives pass by.

RESPONSE Call to mind the face of someone who has been faithful to you in ways that reflect the relationship between Mary and Jesus. Look at this friend with love and appreciation. Consider what his or her deepest needs right now might be. Pray for your sheltering friend and renew your commitment never to leave that person to carry the crossbeam alone.

Dying to Self
◆ FIVE ◆

REFLECTION My grandmother died at the age of 90 in Sacred Heart Nursing Home, a place she had refused to call home for the fifteen years she lived there. We could always count on her to pepper our conversations with a variety of grievances which she had stored away like sugar packets from her tray. Most of them were variations on "I'll never understand why they sold my house right out from under me. I could have taken care of myself." Everyone, including Granny, knew better.

She also made it a point to lament that her roommate was "too snoopy," my mother's hair was "getting terribly gray," my Aunt Vae was "too heavy" and my visits were so rare that she "couldn't remember when she'd seen Gloria last." No one ever took offense. We were glad Granny still had enough spunk to speak her mind.

Whenever she spoke of Hector, who had died nineteen years earlier, Granny betrayed the loneliness for which all of her other complaints were simply a decorative coverlet. She missed her husband, and the years did not allay the loss. But she was no Dickensian Mrs. Gummidge imposing a refrain of "I know that I am a lone lorn creetur" on others. We loved her more for this characteristic reticence on the one burden that really mattered.

At our last visit, I took several photographs of Granny. She is propped up on her bed like an aged bird no longer able to fly or forage. Her sparse hair is permed up in a white crest; her face is etched like an overdone woodcut. I am looking at a dehydrated version of my grandmother, down to the countable bones and the flesh marked by arteriosclerosis and rheumatoid arthritis and the nib of time.

She speaks from photographs as she did on that spring day. Like blind Milton, she dictated lines in which a great effort of composition had been invested. She was beyond complaint and smiling.

"What a beautiful picture you two make together." (These words were addressed to my husband and me as an affirmation of our having overcome our mutual differences.)

"I know they had to sell the house. I couldn't do much even when I was still living there." (She spoke to my mother, who would pass these words on to my aunt and uncle. They would know they were "forgiven" for arranging the sale.)

"I really don't mind it here. The nurses are good to me and it wouldn't be right to complain." (This to all of us with a mere suggestion of suppressed humor.)

She then closed her eyes to rest briefly. We were silent, not wanting to interrupt the flow of her poetry. When she returned to us, her look was distracted. My mother wanted to be sure Granny recognized her eldest granddaughter. "Do you remember Gloria?"

"Oh yes. I've always loved Gloria. And I love her still."

Then, painfully lifting an arm to curve it around my husband's shoulder, Granny said: "After you leave, I'll remember each one of you and how happy I was that you came to see me."

These five "Last Words" remain as my grandmother's benediction and my most valued legacy.

MEDITATION Pain roars through all the outposts of his body, devouring flesh like a fire, breath like a blow. The spikes in wrists and feet have ignited an inferno. He is stretched on a rack, drying out, shrinking up, becoming a whitened carcass. The men who raised him on the tree are pitiless; the tree that will not bend to rest his suffocating weight upon the ground is pitiless; the bystanders who shout "Come down off that cross if you are God's Son!" are bereft of pity.

Jesus is isolated by pain, a pain that has become his world because it is a place no one else may enter. He is aware of a terrible helplessness that has the power to enrage. Unable to pray in words, he prays the pain, wills the connection with Yahweh. He refuses to be destroyed by evil.

Looking down on those who have made themselves his judges and executioners, Jesus says: "Father, forgive them; they do not know what they are doing" (Luke 23:34a).

Bending further to see those who have made themselves his last remnant of compassion and reverence, he says to the one who has loved him from the beginning: "Woman, this is your son" (John 19:26b).

Mary's heart bolts at his voice, which is contorted by the horrible effort to lift the pressure off his chest. The meaning of his last words to her does not immediately penetrate her anguish. But she sees that his glance has turned to John.

"This is your mother" (John 19:27b). He has fulfilled

the final duty of a Jewish son by providing for her after his death. Mary sobs in gratitude and grief as John tearfully embraces her. The two disciples from this moment will be one in heart and mind in everything concerning the legacy of the crucified One.

Now he is more alone than he was in Gethsemane, more alone than when they drove the spikes and drove the tree into the earth of Calvary. He has given everything: his body, his blood, his mother, his life. The isolation wrenches a terrifying complaint from the desert of his heart and mouth: "My God, my God, why have you forsaken me?" (Mark 15:34b).

But God remains silent. Alone, Jesus enters the valley of death. A great cry of protest and submission escapes him. "Father, into your hands I commit my spirit" (Luke 23:46b).

Later Mary will treasure and ponder his last words, knowing that he intended them as a blessing and an inheritance.

R E S P O N S E Stand with Mary at the foot of the cross and listen. Which of the last words holds the most meaning for you? Ponder it in prayer. Decide how you will keep this legacy living and active in memory of him.

THE
GLORIOUS
MYSTERIES

The Arising

♦ ONE ♦

REFLECTION Before our grandchild arrived, I was slip-sliding around on the muddy plateau of mid-life. Even an impulsive return to my alma mater for a graduate degree had not restored my momentum. I never spoke of death, but I feared that it would claim me before I could accomplish anything. I hadn't become a Third World missioner, hadn't written a Great Book—certainly hadn't become the saint I set out to be in my teens. At times I sat like a stone at the bottom of a well, immobile under the weight of regrets and comatose aspirations.

What was it I had lost? Foolish to say "youth," for that was long gone. Better to name idealism, hopefulness and a kind of buoyant spirituality that had kept me under sail in all kinds of weather.

When my son called to ask how I felt about becoming a

grandmother, I made all the appropriate congratulatory sounds, although his announcement hardly touched me. I worried about how the unplanned pregnancy would affect my son and daughter-in-law. I tried on the name *Grandma* and decided it didn't suit me. Addicted to writing and teaching, I considered grandmothering an avocation that would have to be squeezed in between work, study and keeping my husband mildly content.

"At least I won't have any trouble saying no to constant baby-sitting," I assured my friends. They readily agreed, and inquired how my master's thesis was progressing. It was going well. But my head was still under water. I had been holding my breath for so long by then that it felt like my natural state.

The night Kirsten Ann was born we drove four hundred miles through the darkness to be there before her birthday was over. She stunned us with her perfection. Fresh from another galaxy, she radiated an untarnished glory. Everything about her was an intimation of the divine image. We looked at her and the looking felt like prayer. We took turns holding her, greedily absorbing her baby scent and nearly falling over from giddiness and joy. I remembered Thomas Merton's intuition that we are all walking around shining like the sun. Now I knew what he meant.

I had expected someone passive and indefinite as a shadow, an incomplete being who would gradually take her place in our settled lives. Kirsten disdained that role. She came into the world with eyes open and arms stroking like one setting her own course. She seized a place in the center of my existence, carelessly displacing other interests as though they were alphabet blocks. She was so alive that it was painful to observe her.

Ecce infantis! Her mighty arms have rolled the stone from the tomb. She has liberated in me the dormant and self-denied maternal image. I walk out into the sun, anticipating the sound of my name: "Grandma!"

M E D I T A T I O N Delighted with his own radiance, he walks slowly through the garden with the air of a benevolent master. The day is young and open to unimaginable possibilities. Jesus laughs aloud in exultation; he has shed the death mask and trampled on it with impunity. His wounds have been transfigured from marks of humiliation to proofs of royalty. He is the Son, risen and newborn and fully confirmed as Yahweh's own.

In the distance he sees a woman slumped beside the rudely gaping tomb. He can hear her sobbing bitterly like one who has been punished unjustly and sent into exile. His first impulse is to rush to her. But in her terrible bereavement, Magdalene might be deranged by his sudden appearance. She is seeking a dead body, an inanimate object.

Distraught at the sight of two strange beings stationed inside the tomb, Mary focuses only on the barren platform where Christ had been laid. She is in the tomb and the tomb is within her. She died two days ago; her plans and her prayers were unceremoniously buried with her.

The strangers, brilliantly robed and seemingly detached from the reality she suffers, are at least solicitous. "Woman, why are you weeping?" (John 20:13a).

"They have taken my Lord away,...and I don't know where they have put him" (John 20:13c).

45

There is something reassuring in the strangers' smiles that penetrates Mary's desperation. They are like parents who, instead of telling some marvelous news, let their child discover it for herself to her greater gain and joy.

Jesus has quietly approached the tomb and is standing there in gentle triumph. Mary turns slowly, feeling a presence behind her. She is looking into the sun at a man who is mysteriously appealing, but she cannot see him for himself because her mind remains intent on an inert body.

"Woman, why are you weeping? Who are you looking for?" (John 20:15b).

His voice is an embrace. She is shocked at herself for blushing, and at him for using such a familiar tone. What manner of gardener is this?

"Sir, if you have taken him away, tell me where you have put him, and I will go and remove him" (John 20:15d).

He can no longer bear the inward rumble of laughter at Mary's persistence in seeking the dead while confronting the living. "Mary!" (John 20:16a).

At last Magdalene emerges from the tomb.

"Rabbouni!" (John 20:16c).

Giddy with unanticipated joy, she nearly falls on him as she reaches for his radiant face.

"Do not cling to me, because I have not yet ascended to the Father" (John 20:17b).

With a great effort, she drops her outstretched arms but comes as close as she dares to this transfigured Christ, breathing deeply of his fragrance.

Ecce homo! He has delivered her from death and confirmed her identity as a beloved disciple. Magdalene races off to recount the good news to Mary and John, Peter and the others: "I have seen the Lord!" (John 20:18b).

RESPONSE Try to identify any experiences of rebirth or resurrection in your own life. How have they awakened or confirmed your identity? Consider what Mary's response to the resurrection of her Son might have been. Pray that your own capacity for joy at Jesus' rising may expand, pushing aside any stone that may be blocking your faith.

The Glorifying
◆ TWO ◆

REFLECTION Thomas Merton's final pilgrimage led him to Asia and to an accidental death at age 53. His life had been one long, winding, consecrated journey into the presence of the living God—a journey he boldly shared with others through his books. Although Merton was no stranger to suffering, his years as a Trappist monk and hermit prepared him for the complete joy Jesus promised his disciples.

That joy hit Merton between the eyes with the force of a fire hose while he was contemplating several carved Buddhas in Polunnaruwa, Ceylon. These vast stone figures of almost unendurable spiritual beauty triggered a mystical awakening in the beholder. Speaking of the experience in his *Asian Journal*, he says he was wrenched "out of the habitual, half-tied vision of things, and an inner clearness, clarity" seemed to explode from the tranquil Buddha.

Merton, despite his genius for communicating the inner life, was nearly tongue-tied in his attempts to describe what happened to him. Whatever it was, he suddenly realized with immense certainty that "everything is emptiness and everything is compassion." The stone carvings, in their aesthetic representation of unity with God, "spoke" to the monk in a way that pierced through all the layers of subterfuge.

This "beautiful and holy vision" lifted Merton up, filled him with exultation, assured him that he was following the right path. Like Francis of Assisi after he received the stigmata on Mount Alverna, Merton had broken through to a deeper awareness of reality in which all things are intimately connected.

A few days later, after giving a talk at an international gathering of Eastern and Western monastics in Bangkok, Thomas Merton was electrocuted by a fan with defective wiring. The Trappist delegates at the conference later wrote: "In death Father Louis' [Merton's] face was set in a great and deep peace, and it was obvious that he had found Him Whom he had searched for so diligently."

Merton's final words to the monks before leaving the assembly had been: "So I will disappear."

MEDITATION Whenever he appears to them now, he is the morning sun radiating peace. Mary and Magdalene, Peter and John and all his friends are reassured each time he comes again. He is truly risen! He has not left them orphans. Jesus is afire with zeal for the reign of God. And they are slowly, cautiously moving closer to the flame.

Among themselves they are beginning to weave

together the strands of his teaching to illumine a pattern they had not seen before. Mary, like the householder who can bring from her storeroom both the new and the old (see Matthew 13:51), often provides the strands. Like the other disciples, she has not always understood Jesus' words; yet she has always saved them, held them, turned them over and over like precious stones.

Together they assemble the wealth he has given them, interlacing one word with another to discern what lies ahead of them.

> In a short time the world will no longer see me;
> but you will see that I live
> and you also will live. (John 14:19)

> If you loved me you would be glad that I am
> going to the Father.... (John 14:28b)

> ...[U]nless I go,
> the Paraclete will not come to you....
> (John 16:7b)

> Now, Father, glorify me
> with that glory I had with you
> before ever the world existed. (John 17:5)

Now he tells them to remain in Jerusalem waiting for the fulfillment of the Father's promise, for "not many days from now, you are going to be baptized with the Holy Spirit" (Acts 1:5b). Remembering her own prophetic song of victory, Mary is elated at her Son's promise of the Paraclete. She knows that the Spirit of truth will topple the mighty and nourish the hungry and condemn "the prince of this world" (see John 16:11b).

49

The disciples, realizing that Jesus' risen body will soon be taken away from them, spend more time in simply contemplating him. He is the same Jesus, but he is so much more intensely himself that it is impossible to look away from him. He is the Bridegroom, and they are keeping their eyes open while he tarries with them. In silence, they absorb his peace. Unknowing, they are knit together in his love.

He tells them, "[Y]ou will receive the power of the Holy Spirit which will come upon you, and then you will be my witnesses...to earth's remotest end" (Acts 1:8).

When Jesus is lifted up by the Father for his final glorification, the disciples rejoice at this ultimate sign of Yahweh's favor. The beloved Son has carried out all that the Father gave him to do.

For his mother, there is yet a purpose to be fulfilled. The new community, gathered in prayer in the upper room, requires the witness of the first disciples. Mary's pilgrimage continues in the complete joy of one who has seen her Son exalted.

RESPONSE Choose one of the following ways of opening yourself to an encounter with Jesus ascended: Contemplate a Christ icon daily for at least ten minutes. Make a pilgrimage to a shrine, church or religious art exhibit where there is a memorable image of the risen Lord. Meditate on Luke 9:28-36 (the Transfiguration). Ask Mary to draw you closer to her glorified Son.

The Enkindling

◆ **THREE** ◆

REFLECTION We were ground-breakers at the Mercy Sisters' Motherhouse, where fifteen religious women had for the first time chosen a married woman as their summer retreat director. Diverse in ministry, we were one in openness to the new Church as it emerged, squalling, from the birth canal of Vatican II. For five days we had been gathered in prayer and united in seeking the Spirit's guidance.

On the final day we were stirred to rebellion by the July sun and its collaborator, nearby Casco Bay. Like fourth-graders playing hooky, we grabbed picnic baskets and headed for the shore. Our spontaneity prompted new expectations. A line from John ran through my head like a Top 40 tune: "Woman,...who are you looking for?" (John 20:15b). The sisters, in their laughter and allusive smiles, seemed to be hearing the same melody.

We ate and settled like puffins lulled by the waves. The day was splendid. We were figures in a Monet landscape, composed and timeless. Whatever our differences, they dissolved in, to borrow Shakespeare's words, "such harmony [as] in immortal souls."

We began by recalling Sister Francis' discomfort when a born-again Christian had insisted on knowing whether she had been "baptized in the Spirit." He implied that her Baptism in the Church was somehow insufficient. She responded that she had prostrated herself on the carpet and given herself totally, through her religious vows, to Christ. "If that wasn't enough," Francis concluded, "I'm not sure what else I can do."

Then in her mid-60's, Sister Francis had been a teacher for forty years. She thrived in the classroom, nourished by her relationships with young people. Now she had been asked to give up teaching in order to minister to the aged and ill in the Motherhouse. For Francis, the change required another prostration, a new aligning of self with the Shepherd who said: "I lay down [my life] of my own free will" (John 10:18b).

Like Sister Francis, every woman around our picnic table could make those words her own. Each could say, in sincerity: "I lay myself down of my own free will. I have been consecrated in the truth" (see John 17:17) "and my life bears witness to the Spirit of truth" (see John 18:37). "I will seek him whom my heart loves" (see Song of Songs 3:1).

We recalled how we had sung, with flaming faces, at the morning's liturgy, "Set me like a seal on your heart, like a seal on your arm" (Song of Songs 8:6a). The Song of Songs extols a love that is "stern as death" and as consuming as a "blazing fire" (see Song of Songs 8:6b).

We sat, expectant and silent. The sun, like a bridegroom, like a joyful shore-pounding giant, held us. We shared a few lines of a Hindu poem praising Krishna—lines we adapted and redirected to Christ:

> I would set fire to my house for him.
> I would bear the scorn of the world.
> When the sound of his voice reaches my ears it
> compels me to leave my home, my friends.

Commissioned and rekindled anew, we hugged each other and set out in various directions to make whatever "bold proclamations" (see Acts 2:4) our ministries in the Church and in the world required of us.

MEDITATION Mary and the other disciples and relatives of Jesus have come together in the Upper Room to renew their vigil. They are explorers awaiting their Guide; they are shepherds unsure of the new pastures soon to be entrusted to them. Prayer seems the best remedy for the anxiety most of them still feel. Hadn't Jesus insisted that "where two or three meet in my name, I am there among them"? (Matthew 18:20). Hadn't he taught them to pray as a family ("Our Father in heaven..." (Matthew 6:9b), united in their desire for the Helper?

They have been companions at table and at leisure. They have learned to accept, with varying degrees of tolerance, each other's weaknesses; they have become more generous in affirming another's virtue. Following Peter's lead, they have prayed for discernment ("Lord, you can read everyone's heart..." (Acts 1:24b), and chosen Matthias to replace the fallen Judas.

It is the day of Pentecost, the Feast of Firstfruits. The community is expectant. Remembering the first stirrings of the Messiah in her womb, Mary is again prepared to risk her yes to mystery. Of them all, she is least apprehensive for having been tested most thoroughly. She has never taken back her "You see before you the Lord's servant, let it happen to me as you have said" (Luke 1:38b).

They are seated in a circle, at ease in the mutual silence. Gradually a sound like that of wind gathering force over the

Sea of Galilee breaks in on their reverie. The wind, no longer at a safe distance, is now driving through the room with the same mastery Jesus had exerted over the squall at sea.

The disciples, flushed with excitement, have not moved from their places. But, as of one accord, they have linked arms in a gesture of kinship before the Unknown. They are enveloped in the wind which covers them and hems them in like a billowing tent.

Then tongues that appear to be flames part and settle over each of them. At the same instant, each is shot through with the presence of the Holy Spirit, who burns without consuming and transforms without destroying. Mary is ecstatic, recognizing the boundless and unconquerable Spirit of her Son.

Freed from the limitations of their Aramaic tongue, they spontaneously express themselves in languages as foreign to them as the shores of Macedonia. They are walking on water; they are transfigured by jubilation. John whirls Mary around in an impromptu dance, singing "It is his Spirit, his Spirit, his Spirit!"

Recovering themselves and going forth to the crowd assembling outside, they begin making bold proclamations as prompted by the Paraclete. Those who are open to the Spirit hear the disciples speaking an intelligible tongue. Those who are bound by skepticism hear only the ravings of drunkards.

Then Peter recalls to their minds the prophecy of Joel: God will pour out the Spirit on all humankind. God's sons and daughters will prophesy, see visions, dream dreams (see Joel 3:1). Jesus, now exalted at God's right hand, "has received from the Father the Holy Spirit, who was promised, and what you see and hear is the outpouring of that Spirit" (Acts 2:33b).

The new community of believers, enkindled and emboldened, goes forth to work wonders in Jesus' name.

RESPONSE Pray that you may emulate Mary's attitude of openness to risk and trust in the Spirit's power. Then decide how you will make a bold proclamation of your faith in Christ. If possible, make your proclamation (words or deeds) to someone who doesn't "speak your language" when it comes to matters of faith.

The Homecoming
◆ FOUR ◆

REFLECTION Knowing that he would die soon, the 44-year-old man did what came naturally. He sang and required others to sing with him. Francis of Assisi wasn't daft. But he had lived in such a way that death could be befriended rather than feared. Two years before his final illness, the *Poverello* had a vision in which God revealed that his sins would be forgiven and he would be welcomed into his homeland.

Although his eccentric behavior gave scandal to some, Francis refused to spend his last days bemoaning his guilt and beating his breast in *mea culpas*. Instead he composed

a concluding verse for "The Canticle of Brother Sun."
While Brothers Angelo and Leo wept, Francis sang:

> All praise be yours, my Lord, through Sister Death,
> From whose embrace no mortal can escape.
> Woe to those who die in mortal sin!
> Happy those She finds doing your will!

He knew the satisfaction of completing his canticle before
pain and paralysis took over. Then the friars transported
him to the Portiuncula, the little church where they had
known great joy in the community's early years together.

Francis, utterly human and candid to the last, wrote a
message to his lady friend Giacoma di Settesoli, asking her
to hurry from Rome with his favorite frangipani (an almond
and cream confection). Before the messenger could depart,
Giacoma, attendant to her intuition, arrived with the pastry
and Francis' burial garment. The friars attempted to bar her
entry into the Portiuncula, an all-male domain. But Francis
quickly informed them that the lady was "above the rules."
He would not be denied, after twenty years of elected
poverty and hunger, the final pleasure of her company or
her cooking.

Later Francis gathered the brothers and broke bread
with them. He ordered them to remove his tunic and lay him
on the ground in homage to Lady Poverty, whom he had
wed out of love for Christ. Knowing they would long
remember his dramatic gesture, he accompanied it with a
final challenge: "I have done my duty; let Christ teach you
yours."

He blessed each of his followers in turn. They prayed
the Psalms together and sprinkled ashes over their founder.

Francis prayed a few lines of Psalm 141 alone: "Yahweh, I am calling, hurry to me" (Psalm 141:1a).

Hardly able to speak, he attempted to once more sing his praise of Sister Death. And God heard Francis' prayer.

MEDITATION Ever since Jesus' Ascension, his first disciple has been yearning to be reunited with him. As the others have become more involved in the growth and nourishment of the community, Mary has slowly begun to detach herself from her central position as counselor. The disciples have always taken heart at her presence. In her they see not only the physical resemblance to their Master, but the mentor who awakened his zeal for justice when he was still a child in Nazareth.

She has kept his presence before them in a way no other can emulate. Her own experience of rejection by Jesus, who would recognize no claims on him other than those of spiritual kinship, has intensified her discipleship. She first taught him to identify with the lowly as those who were closest to Yahweh; he in turn has instructed her that "Anyone who does the will of my Father in heaven is my...mother" (Matthew 12:50). She raised him to feed the hungry whatever they needed; he corrected her at Cana when she wanted to save the wedding couple from social disaster.

Mary's faithfulness now allows her to anticipate death as a gate that swings open, welcoming her into her Son's immediate presence. Her eagerness is unadulterated by guilt or regrets. She has served him and his friends with all that she had to give. She feels justified in holding Jesus to his promises:

"Whoever believes in me, even though that
person dies, will live." (John 11:25b)

"I am going now to prepare a place for you....I
shall return to take you to myself so that you may
be with me where I am." (John 14:2b, 3a)

"And look, I am with you always; yes, to the end
of time." (Matthew 28:20b)

Her intuition tells her that Jesus, flesh of her flesh, will
soon send for her. In her resurrected body, she will see him
face-to-face. His glory will cover her like a splendid robe;
her humanity will be honored as Yahweh intended all his
daughters and sons to be venerated.

Kneeling at her bedside, John holds her weathered hand
to his cheek. He is trying to let her go without consideration
for his own loss. She is thankful for his smile, grateful that
he does not hold her back by saying "Mother!" Magdalene
too is suppressing her grief as this dearest companion
prepares to go on ahead of the other disciples.

The community gathers around Mary to break bread in
Jesus' name and to prepare themselves for her loss. They
intone those psalms she loves best as a final tribute to her
faithfulness.

Yahweh, be my judge!
I go on my way in innocence,
my trust in Yahweh never wavers. (Psalm 26:1)

God, endow the king with your own fair
  judgment,
the son of the king with your own saving justice.
(Psalm 72:1)

I shall sing the faithful love of Yahweh forever,
From age to age my lips shall declare your
constancy. (Psalm 89:1)

Raising her hand in blessing over each of the disciples,
Mary counsels them to be courageous witnesses to
everything they heard Jesus say, everything they saw him
do. She regards them for some time, then closes her eyes
and begins to sing: "My soul proclaims the greatness of the
Lord..." (Luke 1:46a).

R E S P O N S E Consider how Mary's Assumption is a
call to you to: Reflect on the meaning of your own death;
appreciate the holiness of the human body which, in its
risen form, will endure forever; look forward to your
eventual homecoming and the joyful moment of standing
face-to-face with Jesus, hand in hand with Mary.

The Rewarding

◆ FIVE ◆

REFLECTION If there is any one mystery that has kept me at a cool distance from Mary, it is her coronation in heaven. I have no affinity for queens. Theirs is a life of privilege and idealized femininity; they float while the rest of us thrash around in the murky waters of economic survival, marital trials, vocational doubts and indelible sexism. I am at odds with a Church I think enshrines Mary while preventing other women from rising in accordance with their spiritual gifts.

This traditional image of Mary crowned is barnacled with other troublesome connotations. She is the formidable anti-communist warrior who appears terrible as an army set in battle array. She is the venerated "hail, holy Queen" before whom we "poor banished children of Eve" complain of the earthly misery we must endure as an initiation rite into heaven. She is the fabulous woman of Revelation "robed with the sun, standing on the moon, and on her head a crown of twelve stars" (Revelation 12:1b). These tableaux undoubtedly inspire others; they do not endear Mary to me.

Somehow I had to transform the crown, whether of white roses or gold of Ophir, from an obstacle into a meaningful symbol. I had to see it in a new and more constructive way. Fortunately, three members of the extended family lent me their corrective lenses.

Thomas Merton, who has never failed me in any spiritual quandary, told me, "Try looking at it this way." It's fine to talk about Mary as queen of angels and all humanity. "But this should not make anyone forget that her highest privilege is her poverty and her greatest glory is that she is most hidden, and the source of all her power is that she is as nothing in the presence of Christ, of God" (*New Seeds of Contemplation*).

As I was considering this queen in her unassuming attire, Joan Chittister, O.S.B., boldly lifted me by the nape of the neck and said, "Snap out of it." She couldn't imagine why I hadn't caught on to a more contemporary relationship with the Mother of Christ. "See her as Mary, Queen of Peace...our shelter from war, hatred and oppression...our teacher of peace and justice and reverence for all that God has made" (adapted from *Mary, Wellspring of Peace*).

A more relevant and authentic queenship was emerging. But I still saw the crown itself as a sign of separation, a male-attributed rank of office wedged between Mary and other women. Then, in an article that slipped through my fingers, Robert McAfee Brown made a passing reference to a Latin American celebration of a Marian feast. While praying the Magnificat, the peasants suddenly realized that Mary should be wearing not a gold crown but a straw hat to keep the sun off her face. She belonged less in a cathedral than in a *campesino*'s shack among those her Son favored.

The image of a poor queen in a straw hat humbly teaching justice and peace to those gathered around her drew me on. I was beginning to see her crown as the foreshadowed reward of all who emulate her discipleship.

MEDITATION In honoring his mother and first
disciple, the Son assembles a choir of witnesses who will
speak the word of God as she has lived it. Now in the full
possession of wisdom, Mary will see herself clothed in
peace and crowned with justice. She will experience in her
risen body what awaits the faithful ones whose lives reveal
the glory of the reign of God.

Gabriel: She was deeply troubled by my mysterious
greeting. Yet she neither fled nor protested, but
listened with her entire being. "How can this be?" she
asked, desiring to be faithful both to God and to
Joseph. When I had satisfied this apparent conflict,
she confronted me with courage and said, "You see
before you the servant of the Lord. Let it happen to me
as you have said" (Luke 1:38b).

Elizabeth: When she proclaimed the great Good News to
me, the flames leaped from her to me and to the
bounding son in my womb. She delivered her
prophecy of mercy and justice in a voice that would
have made Herod tremble. For three months, she
stayed with me, filling my ears with Yahweh and
serving my every need.

Joseph: She bore everything—my stubborn refusal to
believe, the censure of neighbors, the rude
surroundings of her confinement—without complaint.
She counted the sorrows of exile a small price to pay
for the child's safety. Even when he failed to
acknowledge her suffering during the three days of his
separation from us, she did not rebuke him. Mary held

her tongue and pondered the words and ways of her Son.

Matthew: When Jesus seemed to reject and disown her by asking "Who is my mother?" (Matthew 12:48b) she did not take offense. She stayed and heard him say, "Whoever does the will of my Father in heaven is my...mother" (Matthew 12:50). From that moment, she surrendered the privileges of maternity and fully accepted her discipleship.

John: At Cana and beneath the cross, she made her just claims on him; he did not deny her. After his Ascension, she became the lamp glowing in the middle of our community, the strong, feminine presence that drew us together in his name.

Peter: She was an example to our flock, an eldress and prophetess and mother, who won for herself an unfading crown of glory.

James: Happy the person who holds out to the end through trial! Once she had been proved, she received the crown of life the Lord has promised to those who love him.

Paul: Just as she, Queen of Apostles, has received a merited crown from the Lord, so have I—and so too will all who have looked for his coming with eager longing.

In honoring his mother and proto-disciple, Jesus gives us a pledge of future glory. Her merited crown is not a sign of

separation or an emblem of unattainable perfection. It is a
bond between us.

RESPONSE Consider how "The Rewarding" or any
of the other mysteries challenges you to be a Mary-like
disciple. How does she call you to be patient when in doubt,
assertive when answers are required, humble in the face of
rejection, prophetic when injustice must be named,
reconciling when peace must be made, strong under the
yoke of suffering, illuminated by the Spirit of unity?
  Remember:

> We make a grave mistake in our spiritual lives
> if she has no part. It is at our peril if we fail to
> understand her role in the life of her Son and in
> our lives. (Paul VI, *Devotion to the Blessed
> Virgin Mary*)

Bibliography

Bishop, Morris. *St. Francis of Assisi.* Boston: Little, Brown & Co., 1974.

Burton, Naomi, Brother Patrick Hart and James Laughlin, eds. *The Asian Journal of Thomas Merton.* New York: New Directions, 1973.

Chittister, Joan, O.S.B. *Mary, Wellspring of Peace.* Erie, Pa.: Pax Christi U.S.A., 1987.

Endo, Shusako. *Silence*, trans. William Johnston. New York: Taplinger, 1980.

Kybal, Vlastimil. *Francis of Assisi.* Notre Dame, Ind.: Ave Maria, 1954.

Merton, Thomas. *New Seeds of Contemplation.* New York: New Directions, 1961.